Y0-ACH-402

rewards of work

growing vegetables

changing

mountains

natural beauty

dreams

soil

wilderness

FARM GARDEN

plant knowledge

wild flowers

solitude

drawing

medicinal plants

life cycles

planning

solace & healing

creating beauty

GARDEN OF MY OWN

layers of soil

drawing

sharing

art classes

puppies

quilting

building work

gatherings

bouquets

A Garden's Echo

H.E. Stewart

Helen Stewart

Cataloguing data available from Library and Archives Canada

Stewart, H. E. (Helen Elizabeth), 1943-

A garden's echo / H.E. Stewart.

ISBN 978-0-9693852-9-5

I. Title.

Manufactured by Friesens Corporation

in Altona, Manitoba, in June 2014

© 2014 by H.E. Stewart. All rights reserved.

PRINTED IN CANADA

Tudor House Press is committed to reducing the consumption of ancient forests. This book is one step towards that goal. It is printed on acid-free paper that is 100% ancient forest free, and has been processed chlorine free.

for my grandfather
William G. Watson

a tender gardener,
a kind and gentle man

Footfalls echo in the memory,
Down the passage we did not take,
Towards the door we never opened,
Into the rose-garden.

T.S. Eliot *Four Quartets*

Introduction and Illustrations

These illustrations are uniquely entwined with their story, a story most unusual in the making. A book pieced together like a quilt of many colours, but without the benefit of any plan or pattern.

In the beginning, a few delicate and detailed water colour pencil drawings encouraged the idea of making more drawings of bouquets, now arranged in special vases painted by my great-grandmother. Scratching into the thick watercolour paper, as with a copperplate for printmaking, added more texture and life to the images. Applying a wash of egg tempera enriched the colour.

While immersed in this art work, I began to search out information about my great-grandmother and then to learn more about my grandfather. I made an amazing discovery – for forty three years, my great-grandfather had been the manager of a nursery large beyond all imagining. It was, in fact, the largest nursery in the world.

I recognized that my interests and talents were part of a pattern, reaching far back in time. This was the beginning of my story and the beginning of this book. I knew that many happy, productive months of work lay ahead. What I did not know was that more and more ideas for flower collages would appear in my mind and that the months would turn into almost three years of work.

I added more layers of colour and texture, turning my drawings into collages. This is a process somewhat like printmaking and, on a grander scale, like creating a garden, itself a richly textured, ever changing collage of plants and trees. For an artist, walking through a garden is to find in nature one small composition after another. For me, creating a book is to use words for connecting one picture to another, an adventure of the imagination and of discovery.

My images grew, as did the story, layer by layer. Old family photographs and more recent colour photos of my own garden were cut, some into tiny bits and pieces, fragments of past memories, now carefully woven into my drawings. These illustrations reflect a timeless, old-fashioned quality. An echo in time, part of a centuries old pattern – a passion for growing flowers, creating gardens, and celebrating natural beauty.

A beautiful garden may still sometimes blossom out of the past. It becomes a pathway back into time, part of an old tradition, a connection to the spirit of nature which continues to live in the garden from generation to generation.

Grandfather's Garden

This story began long years ago, long before my time. It began with my grandmother's mother and her love for painting flowers – and with my grandfather's father and his love for gardening and creating gardens.

I am an artist, with a love for gardening. And this tale began with bouquets from my own garden, bouquets reminiscent of old Dutch paintings, too beautiful to be forgotten. For me, drawing is the best way of remembering – a practice that requires careful study and consideration of small details, watching as the light changes and the petals unfold and fall. It is a pathway to a deeper perception.

The thought of arranging my flowers in the lovely vases, painted by my great-grandmother, was

irresistible. Her pieces were neither superficially sentimental nor typical of the time. My great-grandmother was an artist a century before women were accepted as artists, so she did her painting on fine porcelain. Her Arts and Crafts designs were unusual and imaginative, her colour sense exquisite. Each work is a small treasure of quiet beauty, with the comforting feel of a bygone age.

It is this exact sense of reassurance which comes to mind when I think of my grandmother and the family's two hundred year old home and garden, all held in the hands of a kinder, more gentle time.

When I was still a young child, my grandfather died. Yet he was always a part of my life – and a more meaningful part as time went by.

He was one of twin babies, born so alike that even their mother could not tell which one she held. Their

lives were almost mirror images – their characters, interests and accomplishments strikingly similar.

Just out of business school, on a morning in 1889 the two set out separately to search for work of any type. They soon found jobs as messenger boys in banks, each at a salary of ten dollars per month. Banking was very different then, of course, without the benefit of even adding machines or cheques. Enormous payrolls were transferred from the bank to factories in strong boxes, carried by horse drawn carts and escorted by workers and policemen.

Fifty years later, my grandfather was vice president, and my great uncle president, of their respective banks. The soft-spoken brothers were by then well known for meticulous banking, moral integrity and kindly generosity. Grateful employees planned grand celebrations to honour them and their

long years of service. Messages and congratulations poured in from all across New York state. TIME magazine reported that the modest brothers, "alike as Dromios," went home early after elegant dinner parties at their respective country clubs, "contriving to avoid all the fuss and feathers they could."

Meanwhile, their two banks spilled over with bouquets for the occasion, for the brothers, like their father before them, were known for their love of gardening and cultivating flowers. My grandfather was held in such esteem that for this special anniversary, all employees wore in their lapels a rosebud of pale yellow, my grandfather's favourite, called "Eclipse."

In his garden, many yellow roses flowered. And behind these bushes, more roses tumbled down,

covering high wooden trellises in sweet golden profusion. But as a young child, I favoured the formal rose garden, with its angular raised beds, its fragrant roses of many colours, and its labyrinth of earthen pathways, warm and satisfying to small bare feet. As my grandmother cut roses, I was allowed to pinch off faded pansies. In my childhood mind, this was an important task and a serious responsibility. My grandmother's encouragement would, in time, reap rewards that she never could have imagined.

Every child has their own way of seeing and of responding. Every child creates their own reality. Some have a place that is to them most real, and in their mind, lovely beyond all others. For me, that childhood place was my grandfather's garden, especially at twilight, when fireflies flew about with tiny flickering lanterns.

Early encounters with the larger world of nature may be taken in and subconsciously stored away for later understanding, like the smallest seeds which come to bear fruit long after settling into the earth. Those experiences that resonate with our true selves are remembered with the most clarity, tucked away somewhere in the heart, faithfully waiting to be rediscovered. One fleeting moment can shine outward, while whole years go by almost forgotten. Such experiences may become more significant as time passes. Once in a long while, after deep reflection and introspective examination, they can lead to the visionary insights recorded by mystics, poets and artists.

A love for nature and for gardening must be, in part, a genetic inheritance. I follow after my grandfather, as he followed in the footsteps of his father. And his father, I recently learned, was the general manager of

a nursery on his own street – Mount Hope Avenue in the city of Rochester, New York (the city where I was born). The Ellwanger and Barry Nursery began as a modest seven acre plot, but with enormous hard work, and despite fire and hailstorms, had grown by 1870 to an unimaginable six hundred fifty acres. This was the largest and most respected nursery of its kind in the country, as well as the world.

Immigrants George Ellwanger and Patrick Barry both achieved undreamed success – growing plants, creating gardens and contributing to their community. Both especially loved roses. Ellwanger became a prominent horticultural scientist, with a special interest in hybridizing trees. Extensive experimental grounds made possible such important introductions as dwarf fruit trees. In 1900, the nursery was awarded the Paris Exhibition Gold Medal for its one hundred eighteen pear varieties.

Two hundred fifty well trained gardeners were needed to care for this enormous operation. Large display gardens featured an extensive and diverse selection of ornamentals, shrubs and perennials, flowers and bulbs, at least eighty varieties of peonies alone.

And this nursery was just one of many in Rochester. The great expansion of the gardening business gave rise to various other enterprises. One of the most unique was introduced by publisher D. Dewey, who realized the need for a large scale production of botanical images to use for sales purposes. In 1870, he began printing 'fruit or nurserymen's plates' – lovely lithographs, called chromolithographs, coloured by hand or printed with multiple colour plates. The first images of local plants proved so popular that the choices soon exploded to two thousand four hundred North American varieties.

These prints were sold individually, in portfolios, or as bound collections. They were purchased by nurseries, garden salespeople, horticultural societies and agricultural schools. Travelling salesmen, settling in new places, created their own nurseries, buying stock from Ellwanger and Barry, turning it into a prototype for the nursery industry.

When the demand was at its height, as many as two hundred thousand plates for printing were kept ready at Dewey's company alone. As a printmaker, I cannot begin to comprehend the staggering weight of these materials and the amount of equipment and work space necessary for such tremendous production.

Other lithography companies soon began printing catalogues and seed packets. The early Christian Shakers were the first to sell seeds in paper packets – a small, nifty innovation that made possible huge,

wide-spread sales. In 1838, Charles Crosman left his Shaker colony and founded his own seed company in Rochester, eventually planting one thousand two hundred acres.

As the garden trade flourished, the need for seed companies also grew. A second seed house, Vick's Seeds, filled an average of three hundred orders a day and boasted the largest seed-growing display garden in America. Rochester at this time must have resembled Holland of today, recognized for its unending fields of flowers.

Joseph Harris was the seed house which continued to prosper over time. Trial grounds focused on experimentation – propagating new varieties using the latest systematic and scientific techniques. Eventually the Harris list of hybrid varieties turned into a collection of vegetable super stars.

With nurseries, seed houses and growing numbers of private gardens, is it any wonder that Rochester came to be called "The Flower City," rather than the "Flour City" of earlier days?

By the late 1890s, Ellwanger and Barry's collection of 'flower plates' included a few of the first photographic reproductions. When George Eastman perfected the Kodak camera using roll film, the sale of chromolithographs began to decline as rapidly as it had once spread. Soon Eastman Kodak would become the most well known and prosperous of all Rochester businesses.

The nursery turned to photographs not only for catalogue purposes but for a full record of their large and lovely display gardens. And it is said that Eastman's dissatisfaction with black and white flower photography led to his invention of colour film.

This was a time of close knit communities and a sharing of good fortune. Eastman did that and much more. He used his vast wealth, sometimes anonymously, to help build schools and health clinics in Rochester, but also in other cities. He supported two southern black universities. Still he remained a modest man, passionately devoted to his work.

Ellwanger and Barry also were men of generosity and goodwill. In 1888, they donated twenty choice acres for the beginnings of Rochester's first park, but only with a promise for the establishment of a parks department. There were those who believed that a secluded natural setting would encourage indiscreet behaviour, but in spite of this opposition, Highland Park at last came into being. It was magnificently designed by the great landscape architect Frederick Olmsted. The nursery then offered to donate two of every plant species to any further parks, wisely encouraging the creation of more and more tree-filled spaces.

These two plantsmen (like Giono's *Man Who Planted Trees*) understood the earth's deep abiding need for growing trees. They planted trees near and far, the nearest being just across the road at Mount Hope Cemetery. This was America's first municipal rural cemetery, almost two hundred lovely acres of forests, hills, and valleys. A most peaceful setting for those who died (including my great-grandfather and his family). Perfect also for those who came to visit the graves.

The nursery's trees also lined the city streets, spreading a sense of quiet and stately grandeur as they matured. The gift of countless numbers of trees was perfectly fitting, an inspired legacy of long-lasting beauty.

My great-grandfather's contribution was a passion for gardening, a way of life that encouraged an attitude of respect, modesty and balance. His love of gardening continues on to this day, connecting one generation to another and one garden to another.

Farm Garden

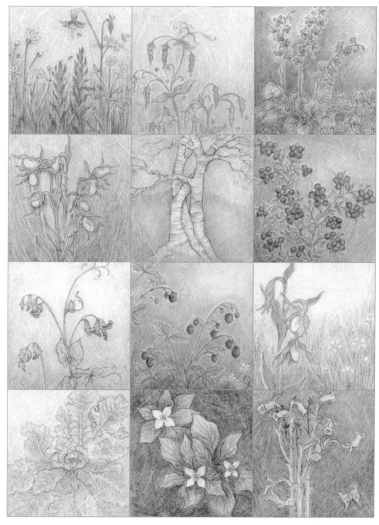

Chapter 2

"I have walked through many lives,
some of them my own,
and I am not who I was,
though some principle of being
abides, from which I struggle
not to stray…"

Stanley Kunitz *The Layers*

Born into a distinguished family, I spent my young life in Berkeley, California, a time when a child could wander about the gentle green hills looking for salamanders and blackberries. From an early age, I attended art school and then studied both art history and painting at the university in Berkeley. I married when I was young and moved to an isolated sheep farm in northern British Columbia – a far cry from home and from what I expected. It was not easy, especially without the skills or training needed for this new living.

Like our farm neighbours, we had to be quite self-sufficient. Working hours were long and winters dark, with deep snows and bitter cold. Even with the constant help of my growing children, the work was never ending and often seemed to me unmanageable. My then husband was teaching at a university many hours away, leaving me much alone with many difficulties, mostly due to my own lack of experience.

In spite of these trying times, I began to appreciate the magnificent beauty of the surrounding mountains and the wildness of the Robson Valley. Our small farm was nestled on a hillside overlooking our fields and the Fraser River – all cradled within rugged, snow-covered mountains. These ancient mountains provided a constant sense of strength and calm in a landscape ever changing. Clouds tumbled down over the peaks, winter snows turned the whole world to white and then melted away, mists drifted over the hills and valley creating shifting patterns of shadow and light, summer storms filled the sky with rainbows of colour. This was a mystical landscape. A masterpiece by the most masterful of all.

Here we worked a huge vegetable garden – virgin topsoil deeply enriched with sheep manure. The good smell of earth and the feel of crumbling soil were like a tonic, all the more because of the terrible cold which came before. Constant weeding gave me the opportunity to watch the plants grow – reaching upwards towards the light, buds opening, leaves unfolding and unfurling, delicate tendrils twining.

Frequent and refreshing thundershowers, combined with long summer days, resulted in produce unequaled for flavour and sweetness. Everything bursting forth and ripening rapidly made it impossible to keep up. An astounding abundance.

Heaps and piles of vegetables. A more tangible and bountiful reward for one's labour could not be imagined. There were, in fact, too many vegetables, far more than we needed. One could not even give them away because neighbours all had gardens of their own.

Like a squirrel stocking up for winter, I filled freezers to the brim and shelves to overflowing. Canning jars spilled over with delicious colours – fruits and jellies, pickles and jams – far more than ever we could eat. This was new work for me and very satisfying. It came to pass that many years later, the tasks were more efficiently routine, but not nearly so appealing.

As summers went by one after another, I loved the garden more and more, the kitchen less and less. I loved the tending of green and growing plants,

my hands working the warm, rich soil, with the comforting sounds and smells of farm-life nearby, and the air itself so fresh and clean. In the garden, I was acutely aware of time passing and seasons progressing. Every day was new and changing. Plants grew quickly, days noticeably longer and warmer. Suddenly it seemed the lush green spring faded into summer heat. And to my surprise, it was not long until leaves turned from green to gold and fell from the trees, leaving their bare branches traced against the sky. And always before our garden work was done, winter set in, often quite unexpectedly.

Yet, when days were warm, when I could work quietly in the garden, time seemed to go by slowly, strangely to almost stand still. The feeling of having enough time for the work at hand was a luxury. On a farm like ours, however, this was a luxury mostly of the imagination.

Occasionally in the summer we walked into the dense forest in search of mushrooms and delicate wildflowers growing in secret sunlit places. More flowers appeared among the long grasses of the hillside fields. The mountain meadows, accessible only by logging roads, were the most glorious, brimming over with wildflowers – a tapestry of colour, alive with butterflies and bees – and mosquitoes by the million.

I had been an artist for many years before my marriage. It never occurred to me that I could ever be too busy for drawing. My awkward attempt at farm work was a questionable substitute for my art work. Creating pictures in my mind was second nature to me, but I still needed to do at least some actual drawing. The only opportunity was usually late in the night – with the huge and silent darkness outside, a time of heavenly quiet after the usual mishaps of the

day. Just once while on the farm, I tried printmaking, unsuccessfully using my treasured wringer washing machine as a press.

In my university classes, abstract painting and self expression had been considered all important. In this northern setting, surrounded by great natural beauty, I returned to illustrating what I observed, especially the world of plants. I studied the structure and growth habits of individual plants, their connection to the soil and surrounding vegetation – an infinitely complex and fragile arrangement, nature's perfect balance necessary for all growing, fruiting and seeding.

My eyes were young and keen and my few drawings intricate and detailed. For many years no one saw these images, but their finely drawn lines,

like those of a spider's web, helped connect me to my surroundings, to a land that began to touch my heart and slowly creep into my soul.

Surrounded by nature, my senses came alive. Some special awareness is lost for me in a busy and crowded place, where technology provides only superficial stimulation and entertainment.

In contrast, living close to the land encouraged dreams of the spirit. Once I dreamed of being buried beneath a favourite birch tree, deep down among the roots, feeling fully at peace. Perhaps this was not a vision of death, as it then seemed to me. Perhaps it was about awakening to a new sense of wonder, more mindful and respectful of the spiritual power of the land itself.

From a wise neighbour I began to learn about medicinal plants. Her family had homesteaded in the valley at a time when there was neither doctor nor provided health care and when plant knowledge was respected. I witnessed some dramatic healing in my own family – comfrey leaves magically knitting together deep cuts, pure honey healing serious burns without scaring, and fresh aloe leaves clearing a dangerous and quickly spreading poison oak rash. (Poison oak did not grow in our valley, but in California where we had just been for a visit.)

The world of plants is indeed a gift beyond measure, like air and water, necessary to all living, but often not appreciated nor properly valued. Plants give us medicines, most of our food – and food also for insects, birds and animals. They provide habitat for all creatures, great and small. They help to hold soil in place and water to seep slowly into the earth. Their dropping leaves and litter contribute to the compost which will, bit by little bit, turn into soil.

Growing vegetation covers the earth in a mantle of loveliness and changing colour, all the while providing the oxygen we need to live and breathe. Remarkable are the workings of this efficient, tightly knit system – beautiful beyond all imagining.

Farm life encourages one to understand these life cycles, to be aware of nature's complexities and the quiet sounds of its beauty – unless, of course, one is too tired or overworked to take notice. Slowly I came to know the rhythm of passing days and seasons, the comfort of solitude, and the pleasure and rewards of hard work.

I would return to this living and understanding later in time, when creating and caring for a large garden of my own.

A Garden of My Own

My own garden began as an idea only, a hoped for dream from the moment I first looked upon our property in Victoria. We arrived mid-winter, after two dangerous days of blizzard travel on snowy, icy roads, followed with relief by an untroubled ferry ride to our new story-book setting. For me, coming to such a place was like coming home. And this home, called Mossy Rocks, was an enchanted place, built as a party house about 1912, set on an acre of rocky outcrop. The property was engulfed by morning glory, brambles, and ivy so deep that it broke apart remnants of rock walls and strangled even the tall firs and lovely Garry oaks. Nearby the ocean spread a sense of calm, as had the Rocky Mountains surrounding our farm.

An early resident had worked for Mrs. Butchart, the remarkable gardener who turned her husband's cement plant and abandoned limestone quarry into lovely gardens. This employee preferred creating his own "little Butchart Gardens" at Mossy Rocks. Seventy years later, just the faintest trace of such a garden remained. I knew at once that it could again be beautiful.

My children made tunnels through the tangled growth, built tree houses and sometimes helped root out the ivy. We continued working our farm during the summer months, but this shortened season resulted in an ever more frantic pace and left little time or energy for a garden in Victoria. My husband was more and more away, travelling in his own world of adventures, until I was alone, this time for good. I turned to printmaking, giving art lessons – and to gardening.

Our property was rocky, with only a thin layer of soil, very different from our farmland. Collecting chips seemed appropriate – shredded trees and leaves, free for the taking. I studied gardening books, pored over catalogues, and walked with my little daughter in public gardens and the Butchart Gardens. It pleases me now to know that many of Mrs. Buchart's foundation plantings must originally have come from Ellwanger and Barry.

I visited nurseries and often took my young daughter to look at the plants. This was a new, unexpected pleasure, and deeply satisfying. I can imagine my grandfather's delight as a child visiting his father at the greatest nursery of all. And I can imagine my great-grandfather working at such a nursery, choosing plants to take home for his own garden, his cup of happiness filled to overflowing.

I have always liked the making of things. To create something of beauty, especially during periods of unsettling difficulty, provides a sort of balance, a comfort and healing. Creating a garden gives one a healthy purpose and a sense of oneself. More than one blessing is granted if the land is healed, along with the gardener.

My own story now turned once again to my grandfather. Like a gift from heaven, his unlooked-for legacy provided the means to begin repairing our tumbled-down home and to plant a garden.

One good fortune followed another. I met an energetic and gifted gardener, happy to take on my acre of property, consisting as it did of enormous heaps of shredded chips. Eighty-five huge truck loads full, sprinkled with nitrogen and falling rain over two winters to encourage decomposition.

Considering both the position of the house and the playful habits of my puppy, we quickly marked out (with a shovel) an unexpected, unusual pathway. Next we began to bring in rocks, which was to me even more astonishing. From nearby blasting sites, big trucks dumped off piles of rocks, somewhere between one hundred fifty and one hundred eighty tons in all. With much enthusiasm, my gardener began to weave these large rocks together, lining the pathways and creating huge planting beds. A massive undertaking, this was unlike any gardening I had ever known.

To move the largest rocks and to pile chips into the beds, a kind neighbour helped with his backhoe. My two youngest children cheerfully joined in, moving hundreds of wheelbarrows of material from one place to another. Topsoil, also by the truckload, was dumped off, then piled onto the chips for the

planting of trees and shrubs. Many of these came from specialty nurseries and were chosen with care, only those plants that I wished to draw. (To the dismay of many, mine is a rhododendron-free zone. I prefer more subtle blossoms, like those of mountain wildflowers.)

In my mind's garden, I had imagined myself as a zen monk, meditatively raking my gravel paths among the rocks and trees. Instead, these pathways quickly sprouted more seedlings and weeds than any of the beds. Over time, the children helped to cover all of the pathways with a mixture of cement, sand, gravel and soil. I pressed bricks, pieces of slate, ferns and different designs, into this wet concoction. Our efforts were well rewarded, for my weeding time was greatly reduced and the whole garden now more manageable.

Our years working together on the farm provided excellent training for this great task. It was in some ways like farming again, but this time by choice and without need to toil on endlessly or to work when the weather turned very cold. I was still young and strong enough to enjoy every minute.

Every garden reveals some aspect of the gardener's personality and past experience. My own garden was inspired by my grandfather's garden and by the beauty of northern wilderness. My grandfather's was a formal garden, with straight pathways and bare ground. It had been cultivated for so long that hardly a weed survived for seeding. The soil, deposited by a giant glacier, was deep and rich in nutrients and minerals. His was a tidy garden. Early Christian settlers, especially such sects as the Shakers, believed that gardening was God's work. A well ordered garden was a reflection of an orderly mind.

Mine is not such a garden. It is more of a natural, working garden. It is also a relatively new garden, filled with weed seeds and juicy morning glory roots, but also happy, fat worms. I am gardening on top of bedrock. Constant mulching is necessary to increase and enrich the soil, to help retain moisture and to slow the growth of weeds, a practice even more valuable as the world of sensible seasons changes and the weather no longer behaves in predictable ways.

A responsible gardener is one of the earth's caretakers. This still seems to me like God's work, perhaps more important today than in the time of our forefathers, because so much land has been lost – either covered over or grossly contaminated. I want to care for my small piece of ground in the best way I can. The act of gardening provides a direct experience of beauty, touch and smell. At the same time, it connects us to our subconscious inner self,

and may therefore eventually lead to a more intuitive and spiritual understanding of the earth. Gertrude Jekyll, the most influential and inspired of early women gardeners, believed that gardening could be a road to redemption. If everyone today could plant and tend some flowers or carrots, the world would regain a bit of balance.

My garden has been a communal effort. In the beginning, I was merely watching, learning and helping. But over many years now, a host of workers have helped me and all have benefited in different ways from the gentle and kindly spirit that resides here, as have the large numbers of visitors over the years. I like sharing my garden and my home. This has become a gathering place for parties, dances, charity events, art classes and concerts. At any time of year I am able to pick bouquets for drawing or for giving away.

Twenty years after its beginning, the garden is mature and more lovely than ever. It continues to change, more quickly than I would have thought, and I keep working and planning for these changes.

Gardening is a way of life, almost like farming. I am outside nearly every day and have been for many years. I try not to be always working, but sometimes just to walk about, checking on the plants, watching and listening for nature's spirit shining through, echoing like a heartbeat. Small garden compositions, like ever-changing paintings, can be mesmerizing. In late summer, my large, sweet-scented lavender bush trembles with insect life – bumblebees, fuzzy yellow, black, and cream coloured, and various honeybees and a dusting of tiny orange skippers. These little butterflies determinedly skip from flower to flower, darting and dancing, then suddenly pause to rest, opening their folded wings as if to absorb the warm sun.

And always nearby in the garden, one of my bearded collie puppies has been with me. Theirs is a blissful world for playing, chasing balls and squirrels, rolling on the grass, and sleeping in the shade. It is also a good place to die. The last one is buried with the others, deep in petals of Cecil Brunner roses. I would like such an end myself, not under northern birch trees, but in my own garden, covered over with rose petals.

71

On his mystical journey, Stanley Kunitz heard a voice directing him. *"Live in the layers not on the litter."* As a gardener, this glorious poet knew about composting and layering. His own garden had grown gradually, changing from sand dunes into flower beds.

The earth also was created layer upon layer. Fallen leaves, needles, twigs and dried grasses, all decomposed, ever so slowly, creating one inch of precious topsoil every one hundred years. My garden is now many layers deep, richer by far than when I began working. I have had the great advantage of hauling in piles of mulch, truckloads of grass clippings, manure, and tree trimmings already chipped and shredded.

Much of the world, however, is not faring so well. In many places, layers of plastic and toxic waste are choking both land and water. *Whatever are we thinking?* We can no longer move on to greener pastures, having destroyed those of the past. My grandfather's home was eventually demolished, his lovely garden ripped up to be replaced by a parking lot, a deeply painful progression, not only for the family, but for the beautiful soil, now tragically dry and dead beneath the pavement.

As early as 1877, Gerard Manley Hopkins wrote his concern and sadness for the earth. The conclusion of his magnificent poem "God's Grandeur," still sets one's spirits soaring.

"And for all this, nature is never spent;
There lives the dearest freshness deep down things;
And though the last lights off the black West went
Oh, morning, at the brown brink eastward, springs –
Because the Holy Ghost over the bent
World broods with warm breast and with ah! bright wings."

But these words were written before the time of clearcut logging, wide-spread polluting, over-fishing and fish farming, oil drilling, strip mining, fracking and heaven knows what else. What would he feel today, when much of humankind seems almost intent upon the earth's destruction? One must wonder how long the Holy Ghost will remain patient and protective.

We shall not cease from exploration,
And the end of all our exploring
Will be to arrive where we started
And know the place for the first time.

T.S.Eliot *Four Quartets*

Deep down in its layers, the earth holds memories of the past. So too, it is with gardens. The land remembers. The gardeners' work and care filter down into the earth itself, and in walking in an old garden, we may hear the gentle sound of their footfalls from times gone by.

Planting a garden is an act of faith, even if no garden is forever, just as no life is forever. We do the best we can to make it worthwhile, to make it beautiful and meaningful, hoping that some of that effort may continue on. In the end, the hopes and dreams of one age may die but be reborn at a different time and in an unexpected place. The heart of a garden will then live on, echoing times past.

Still round the corner there may wait
A new road or a secret gate
And though I oft have passed them by
A day will come at last when I
Shall take the hidden paths that run
West of the Moon, East of the Sun.

J. R. R. Tolkien *Roads Go Ever On*

BOOKS OF INTEREST

Green Thoughts   Eleanor Perényi

The Wild Braid   Stanley Kunitz

Dear Mr. Jefferson   Laura Simon

The Morville Hours   Katherine Swift

The Education of a Gardener   Russell Page

In My Garden   Christopher Lloyd

Onward & Upward in the Garden   Katharine S. White

American Garden Writing   edited by B. Marranca

The Inward Garden   Julie Moir Messervy

Arts & Crafts Gardens   Wendy Hitchmough

Antique Flowers   Katherine Whiteside

The Shaker Herb & Garden Book   Rita Buchanan

The Making of a Garden, Gertrude Jekyll
   anthology compiled by Cherry Lewis

The Man Who Planted Trees   Jean Giono

200 Years of Rochester Architecture & Gardens
  Richard Reisem

For the Love of a Rose   Antonia Ridge

The Man Who Painted Roses   Antonia Ridge

In Search of Lost Roses   Thomas Christopher

The Paper Garden   Molly Peacock

Mrs. Delany and Her Circle
  edited by M. Laird & A. Weisberg-Roberts

Berkeley to the Barnyard   H. E. Stewart

The Sweetness of a Simple Life
  Diana Beresford-Kroeger

Second Nature   Michael Pollan

Beatrix Potter's Gardening Life   Marta McDowell

In and Out of the Garden   Sarah Midda

Tree and Leaf   J. R.R. Tolkien

TreeSong   H. E. Stewart

With much appreciation

to **Patrick Hauser** for his generous
contribution to Tudor House Press

to **Chris Ball**, devoted gardener and
excellent teacher

and to **Lorna Janz**, best of book designers

Special thanks also to my good friends

Carolyn Wade, Karen and **Michael Prince,
Viveka Janssen**

and my daughter **Sarah Stewart**

for their encouragement and insightful suggestions